# Logjam

Also by Arthur J. Stewart

*Rough Ascension and Other Poems of Science*

*Bushido: The Virtues of Rei and Makoto*

*Circle, Turtle, Ashes*

*The Ghost in the Word*

*From Where We Came*

*Elements of Chance*

*The Hallelujah Series and Other Poems*

*Uncoils a Snake: A Poetry Chapbook*

# Logjam

by Arthur J. Stewart

Periploi Press

NASHVILLE, TENNESSEE

2022

*Design by Dariel Mayer*

Manufactured in the United States of America

ISBN: 979-8-9857833-0-8

A logjam is a naturally occurring phenomenon characterized by a dense accumulation of tree trunks and pieces of large wood across a vast section of a river, stream, or lake. Logjams have ecological value.

—*Wikipedia*

# Contents

# Preface and Acknowledgments

*Logjam* is a collection of longish science-inspired poems. I use the term longish here by intent. While none of the poems in *Logjam* are as long as many famous long poems, such as "The Song of Hiawatha,"[1] or "Garbage,"[2] or "Rime of the Ancient Mariner,"[3] all of them are longer than many famous short poems, such as Robert Frost's "Fire and Ice," or William Shakespeare's 14-line beauty, "Shall I Compare Thee to a Summer's Day?" So the term longish seems appropriate. In any case, a poem should be just long enough to effectively say what the author is trying to say, and no longer. Hopefully, the poems in this collection meet that criterion.

In her essay titled "An Anatomy of the Long Poem,"[4] Rachel Zucker notes that "a long poem isn't just a short poem that the poet forgot to end." Rather, it is a different kind of horse altogether: the long poem "embraces and rejects and re-embraces imperfection." Long poems "require and inspire a different mindset, a different pacing, a different way of being, a different kind and level of intimacy with another person and with the self." Both in literary disciplines and in scientific disciplines, relative comparisons, such as short versus long, are fraught with contextual ambiguity. A million years is long compared to a human's life-span, but it is a mere blink of the eye compared to the estimated age of the universe—some 13.8 billion years or so. And an ant may be small to us, but monstrously huge compared to a bacterium. Yes, longish is the right word.

Practically, I've found it can be difficult to get longer poems published because they take up more space and publishers often prefer to include more items, with good diversity in the limited amount of available space. Who wants to read one long poem when three well-crafted shorter poems might be included instead? So, over a longish while—about twenty-five years or so—I accumulated a set of largely unpublished longer poems. Now, following my 72nd birthday, it seems time to clean out the garage: time to un-jam it.

Each of my previous books of poems has been strongly themed. With tongue in cheek, I can say that the theme for this collection is poem length—by their presence, these poems collectively address the question, how long is long enough? Except for the opener, none of the poems here is shorter than 111 lines, and the longest contains 459 lines. And each poem in this collection incorporates, at some scale, a consideration of time-length. Time, after all—and perhaps hope—is all we really have. And actually, we just borrow time: we don't have it.

The reference to science-inspired poems, noted in the first line of this preface, should not be neglected, either. The science-inspired vocabulary, topics, images, and perspectives invoked in *Logjam* become evident quickly, and they persist as a result of my forty years of experience as a practicing aquatic ecologist. When one is embedded in a profession for that length of time, there's scant alternative: each professional area develops its own distinctive language, in part as a professional group-bonding mechanism. As an experiment, try reading an article in *Science* magazine, and then try reading a lawyer's brief: the terms, the length and structure of the sentences, the acronyms, and the concepts reveal huge differences. Thus, the science aspects of the poems in this collection of necessity shine through. I hope you will enjoy them.

Special thanks to Jim Johnston, who reviewed and commented on an earlier draft of *Logjam*. His guidance was superb.

"Righteous Things" was first published in *Consilience Journal*, Issue 8, under a CC BY-NC-SA license.

Two additional poems in this collection—"Red Lady"[5] and "From Where We Came"[6]—have been published previously. "Red Lady" is republished here with verbal approval of the anthology's lead editor, Margaret Britton Vaughn. "From Where We Came" was first published in *Cultural Studies of Science Education.*

To get warmed up, let's start with one short, stubby poem.

REFERENCES

1. H.E. Longfellow. 1855. *The Song of Hiawatha.* Reader's Digest Association (January 1, 1989). 350 p. ISBN-13: 978-0895773371.

2. A.R. Ammons. 2002. *Garbage.* W. W. Norton & Company. 121 p. ISBN: 0-393-32411-7 pbk.

3. S.T. Coleridge. 2015. *The Rime of the Ancient Mariner.* Andesite Press. 92 p. ISBN: 78-1502451057.

4. R. Zucker. 2010. "An Anatomy of the Long Poem." https://poets.org/text/anatomy-long-poem

5. M.B. Vaughn and S. Alfred. 1996. *Southern Voices in Every Direction.* Bell Buckle/Iris Press, Bell Buckle, TN. 159 p.

6. *Cultural Studies of Science Education*, DOI 10.1007/s11422-014-9624-x.

# Logjam

# Logjam

Big logs, with bark on or bark
skinned off; rough
water flowing under and

partly over, making the sound
of dark water sucking
wet wood, everything

slippery, almost in balance —
trunks, heaving this way and that, some
with limbs, some with limbs

sawed or snapped off. Get the peavey going,
work it hard; be careful
where you step.

# Not Some Other Place

1.

We can be scared of being scarred
or scarred from being scared. It all
works out circular, you see — but put an upward
push and a spin on that and it becomes

cylindrical: and since nothing is
more perfect than a circle, conical
is next in line: comical, isn't it:
could stand there, scratch

the head in consternation, but that
action's not productive because
it is what it is. Look, like Archie said, you'll find
nothing lowly in the universe —

even the lowest microbe
is a wondrous thing
of beauty, fancy that.

2.

And atoms. Amazing
how several in a group can tunnel
out from an energy well faster
than the speed of light: sheer delight

in how they sparkle oscillate and spin. Note
the commonality here is spin: a
rotational motion — from large, such as
Earth around sun, or sun around

the center of the Milky Way
galaxy, or heading down, moon

around Earth, Earth
on axis, then five huge gyres

such as North Atlantic and North
Pacific, among others, and
within those fleas are other fleas:
large whirly winds that churn

north or north and east unless
another way is better. Go
figure. Tornados
are so much smaller

in comparison

3.

And the water-gyres: well,
some surface matter floats
by definition, so much is
swept up, harvested

and concentrated by the push
of surface water moved by wind
and gravity and spin: see,
right back

but on land the spin
makes different things different: con-
sider the moon, rising fatter night
by night then going

the other way; con-
sider the up and down or in and out
of tides, the glows
of the Aurora Borealis or

its southern equivalent: the mind
boggles: magnetic spin
spins bait troll, draws and twists
the thing to yarn: fabricate

by processes of
imagination. Futile. Wheels.
Spinless is close to spineless
in some dictionaries. They should do

something about that.
Okras for example

4.

Ok, Ok, e-
nough of that. Some time ago, a random circle
grew to become a sphere: fully
swollen to perfect dimensions, ex-

panded as much as possible but
more a bauble than a bloated bead because
the latter has connotation of a mess
whereas baubles do not: they just

sparkle, glisten. When a fiddlehead
fern begins it begins as a tetrahedral
spore that becomes
a gametophyte and the gametophyte

releases eggs and sperm and
you know what happens then: they
get together, unite and the com-
posit thing grows into the larger

body, the sporophyte phase
of the fern, and there
on the undersides of the fronds, small brown
circular places develop where new spores

form. Like, the form
of a motion. * And dew
on fronds. There's a dozen ways

to get there from here. A little rain
usually increases humidity, and that
also favors ferns

5.

Bought a new oil painting today and boy
it is a beaut: not so special with respect
to subject, the usual
trees along a stream but wow!

the sycamores are clearly sycamores
with their distinctive raggedy-ass bark
and they're living
right where they're supposed to,

leaning over along the bank:
no out-of-placeness for those guys,
they positively know
where to be and when and where the water is.

And good soil. But wall space limits:
we'll need to jam
something somewhere to make things fit.
Crammed or not, still a beaut.

6.

Back to painting: father artist once
smashed a lovely work in a fit
of rage and I was
morally outraged — art

when made does not belong
to the artist but to
those outside who see: he had no right
to do that: I was young

enough to cry
almost like standing
on the stump or there
by the road where the mishap occurred.

That's enough.

7.

Could go back
to donkey-land: in Arizona; a fenced-in
place along a canal of the
Roosevelt Irrigation District

and we being kids would
sometimes sneak in, rope
a burro, fetch it out and ride,
usually to the neighboring ranch

where we'd steal
a big watermelon on a hot day;
kept it under a wet
gunny sack to cool and later ate

the thing, delicious red, spitting
black seeds here and there far
as possible. Then we put
the donkey back, not even

a watermelon-bite for him: shame.
We knew better and
probably he would have liked it

8.

But that's past too.
As are other places: but still I feel I need
to knead the time of another time, not just
knuckle a different place, over

and over, home or not home. It's time
to check the clock and see
the twitchy second-hand tic; see
the moon swell or shrink sliver by sliver,

and monitor at night cold stars
that seem to move not a whit except
together: I don't have enough time:
motion or no, not enough time

to spin forward an arrow of time:
fletched, notched, the bow's strung tight

9.

As a bicolored kite tugs hard
against a windy day, the wind
surging and declining, gusting
now and again against

a raw blue day: the yellow and
red taut body whirling sometimes as a
gust pushes hard the kite whirling because
the tail then (for that moment) should be

longer: a white series of knots,
narrow strips tied of old bed-sheet,
the body whirling and the tail
whipping almost in a circle

until the gust damps and things
right themselves again,
head up, proud, joyous.

10.

Like water: water knows
important things to know: it responds
properly to gravity, physical ob-
structions, temperature,

even to dissolved salts: it holds
ions at just
the right distance, according to
their individual charges; surface

films can slide over the surface
at the slightest touch of
wind; water-striders
dimple the surface but do not

fall through; minnows glitter
as they scrape green from the surfaces
of submersed stones; or find
small living things

to eat. In the water-world
they, too, get enough
to make do, somehow
enough to make do.

Warmer water floats
on cooler water; sunlight
penetrates as far as it can before
it is burned out, before

it dissipates and in so doing
photons are absorbed, con-
verted to
molecular motion: jiggle

faster, random motion becomes
what we call heat. This
all sounds so boring.
And it is, but it is

significant, too. Perhaps
gaze more
at art or logs.

11.

Because
it's just a thread and a thread
will wobble away
by itself sometimes

under twist or pressure: so
if you want it, hook it firmly first
to a twig or limb, something
that can withstand a gale.

Mountains of time ago
men in a broad sense
lived peacefully, ripping out
hearts and livers

of prey but mostly
leaving other humans alone:
except the Aztecs, the Mayans, and dozens
of other groups, tribes, units,

gatherings, collections — all manner of
congregations, similar or dis-
similar, depending upon
criteria used to judge.

Yet we've been told to judge not.
Go figure.

12.

In any case we're here
now and not some other place:
it matters not the form, the
picky style or sticky pile, the shape,

the weaky squeal, the direction
of up or down or spin: I see
outside that overnight
a dense fog has frozen to a hoary frost:

it spangles every twig and limb.

13.

A gloomy gray today. It's
mid-January and from the past
one might anticipate a mid-month thaw:
a week-long warm, but

no, according to reports
it's going to go the other way.
Took the dogs
yesterday to the park along the creek

on leashes and they pulled
me along like mad but stopped
here and there to smell the smells:
they so like

to sniff things up; there must be
ten thousand smells to smell
if you're doggish but it was
still a good walk for them and me.

That's a place too: along
the creek, mostly the water
is clear and quickish, running
over the bed not languorous and slow;

the pools when there are pools are
shortish, deepish, rockish and you can
hear the water rushing
from rock to rock, too swift

for some kinds of
minnows but good for
others: logperch, perhaps,
a darter or two: they like

faster water and dash out
from behind a shielding rock to snag
a bug or two: water too quick
for stone-rollers, the males

of which hunker down, yes, in riffles
in spring but larger schools prefer
larger, deeper pools. I enjoy watching
schools of stone-rollers feed in pools; their

smooth bodies twist and flash in sunlight as they
feed on algae they scrape from rocks.

14.

And around another bend, gradient
still too steep to allow
large pools: the dogs have finally
pulled me back

to the truck: loaded'em up, un-
snapped the leashes, took them
not to some other place
but home.

15.

Lately I've discovered need
to reconcile: a need

to make things fit, a need to make
meaning when I can from

small unrelated things: my life
is creeping along, not well
justified; I'm not
using much of what I've learned

so it seems a waste. What if
the heavens opened up and
revealed Truth or offered
everlasting life; it might be

terrible: everything
I've done and learned
to now would be made
useless:

a good thing I'm on
an antidepressant, eh?
But oh well
again. Next week I go

on-line by Zoom to instruct
a dozen science interns how to
use the Web of Science: it's a fine
tool. Sometimes

separately from teaching I drag out
William Carlos Williams, his
Selected Poems * and
read a few, scattershot to get

the feel; he was so good
with imagery: I've flagged

The Mind Hesitant and
To a Solitary Disciple and re-

fuse to abuse
his book with dog-ears; un-
leash the term observe
or rather grasp: that's what it takes

sometimes to reconcile

16.

the dogwood tree
outside my second-floor
office window
sports tight pinkish buds,

swollen nodules, each
a little fist on the tip of almost
every twig: when blossoms
roar out this spring

it should be a dandy show:
the leaf buds in contrast are
more slender, far more
delicate:

and sure, as WCW re-
ports, avoid bland colors, focus
instead on place, shape,
contrast and especially

just observe and ex-
press, perceive,
observe, express.

17.

Today the brother of a
high school football coach in a small town
not far from here died
of Covid and the coach

died too, a week earlier,
as did their mother; just about
the whole family, damned near
wiped out just like that:

it doesn't seem fair, probably
they were all
good people, as many people are:
even bad ones

almost always have at least
a little good and sometimes
a lot. But it is
difficult to know because

there are so many people, some
this way, some
that way, sharing
certain things and keeping

certain things private. Take
things offered and offer
thanks; give
things you can give and don't

worry about getting thanks,
the world probably would be-
come a better place
overall: it's just

judgment that makes
things seem so awkward. That's
an interesting word with two w's
not so far apart and awkward

is not just somewhat difficult to
spell, it also clutters up
things that naturally want to
happen. With

awkwardness: I go
more often with discomfited
or maybe gawky
thinking about turkeys: they're

pretty funny birds

18.

in a pen or free-
ranging, pea-brains; don't know enough
to come in out of the rain but
still they thrive

in the wild, outdoors: wily birds;
if not smart ungainly if you
ask me but the hens with their
big broods are still cute

in spring. The hen
nests on the ground, incubates
her eggs day and night while the toms
take to the trees at night, come down

out of the trees early each day
sort of a division
of labor or spreading risk but
not many of the chicks make it

through the first month. We do
a lot better or worse than that
depending on your criteria. There's a long
list of critters that enjoy

turkey eggs or young turkey chicks;
it's such a hard world
even in the best of times:
seems like not much

piping of plenty although
in fact there is

19.

plenty. Almost enough
to go around, if you scratch off
places where famines are under-
way, and places

where there just isn't
enough food to go around, or
not enough water, so
malnutrition is rampant: like

we have too much here and
not enough there, if there was only
a way to smooth it out more,
just a way to make things

you know, more equitable: wouldn't that
be OK? Isn't that something
we should try to do? I don't have

an idea about how to make things move
in that direction, spin or no, circle,
oval, up or down. But I do observe
we're here

and not some other place.

20.

Could skip this but
twenty seems better than
some uneven number: that's
just my opinion

WHY NOT GO FOR IT

21.

When the suet goes out
the birds come in: the titmice,
a downy woodpecker, a yellow-
shafted flicker, the inevitable

blue jay and yank-yank
head-down white-breasted
nuthatch: they relish the
suet-embedded corn, millet,

sunflower seed: and last, a gray squirrel
sprawls the suet cage, wanting

the whole thing. Last year one learned
how to open the basket; the whole block

fell out, the dogs
took over. The calories,
that's what they need: the little bodies
of the birds require calories;

they work hard to stay alive;
hang around
when the weather grows cold.
And windy today. The wind

blows off the little heat they have,
makes one hope
for spring: huddle up
like a bird and hope.

22.

Another pull-job
in the park today; I can make the leashes
short or long as needed, so I
shorten them as we approach

other people, because our two mutts
have no social skills — they jump
up, front paws out, tails
wagging hard to lick a face and if

the passer-byer also has a leashed
dog, mischief can happen fast
and our two dogs pull like mad, seriously
wanting to investigate

at depth. One of the two
is a chunky Catahoula mix, with
some bull-dog looks and traits;
she's got a whoppered ear

blue cracked glass eyes and talks
almost constantly, but has little to say.
The other is larger, a deer-brown
Appalachian cur, white blip on tail-tip, bred

in this area, near this place, over generations
for hunting; she's dangerously strong.
And clever. Guess which one's a slow-
sniffer: takes her sweet time evaluating

fully the complex
medley of novel odors retained
on the grass
and here and there at the bases of

lampposts, trees, split-rail
fence posts; the other one just
sniffs and goes, sniffs and goes; not
sure how I can teach them to go on walks

without them pulling so hard;
I'll need to look it up. They say
there's more to matter than what
it does to gravity

23.

whirling
or spinning dervish-like or slower
I could point repeatedly to this thing
or that: object

or agree to this thing
or that, give purpose or
if not give purpose then
give state or sense, opinion

at least, view estimation; be-
lief, judgment but I hope
not that: more towards
attitude, a positive reflection

yet at day's end such things
are so fragile; not brittle exactly
but delicate, not
crumbly but in-

substantial: wispy, pre-
carious but precious; when
my life closes, bookish, pages
thumbed and marked

but not dog-eared: it's OK, I'll
prowl another nearby hill: not
some other place; peer over it and
re-view below a hawk's solo tilt on a

warm cloud-free summer day's
rising column of air.

# Being Human

In these bedraggled times, time
has scant meaning: I'm properly in the moment
for a moment, but then I slip

quick and slick as a tweet, the mental feet
start dancing by themselves — toes in, toes out,
jiggle the shoulders, tilt

the upper half of the bod but
let's just say stop.

   Stop.

With the glut.
Stop

moving the glutes. One could work to perform
each of the seven deadly sins — make a plan
and work it. Pride, for example. Purpled
mountains of pride; high school Panther Pride,
Black Pride, Proud
boys with trinket toys, wannabes but
it can surge like an artesian well until

    Just.
      Stop.

There's a greasy slope
to coveting: the wanting, the
hankering, yearning, craving, the long
longing for. Smear it
like apricot jam on fresh warm bread, like slow
honey, lick
the lips, the soft little nubbin, the spoon
    after or before.

And then there's lust. A must of lust, in fact.
But how does lust differ
from coveting? The wanting, the
hankering, yearning, craving, the long
longing for. Universal, a core

of being, a misty must.

One can anger at the surge; auger the source
through gravel-down, become ear-
itated at hearing
words you don't like. Like, you know, you should —

well screw that. It awl works out to no good;
get auger it: turn uber
a new leaf, often
anthrocyanically reddish first and radish later.

Bringing one to gluttony: think muttony, the fatty
blood-red juices
best; stewed or roasted or in some way

cooked: like your goose
when your ego gets in the way. Eating
to excess. Gluttony couples
tastefully to greed. Which as a word
rhymes with weed seed treed breed creed,
the works. Make a mash-up, e.g. squeeze
out and save
the juice. But not loose. Rather,
it gets tight around the belt-line: a true
signal of too much. What about

envy: seems like coveting, close to lust
but maybe the objective of the thing —
you know, differs a little, like a
shadow or a silhouette in dim light
makes a sure trajectory difficult. Craving

something another person has:
now there's
irresponsibility incarnate. Broad-beamed

error. Oh, I am so

envious of what you have. Oh,
I covet that thing, I long-lust

that which you have and which I think
I do not have, or I think I do not have
enough of.  I could want

wantonly
for that thing I think I don't have until
exhausted: tired out, and sloth

takes me over. In Costa Rica
we saw sloths
of two types, one rarer than the other

        which is
inevitable, an inevitable
condition. Almost hidden
among sun-spangled leaves in tall trees
bending over the road; slow-

moving, one patient
reach after another
with two or three toes. By comparison

I write ferociously in retrospect,
pointing all ten fingers
incessantly to the future.

# Red Lady

*Red Lady Goes to Church*

I start this poem with a white lady in a red dress.
She is divided, top to bottom, by a wide black belt.
In autumn all curves she moves, a sleek
fox in crisp black shoes; in light they glisten.

By themselves they seem to move her. Listen:
up the sidewalk — clack, clack, clack, clack.
They carry her across the walk.
They move her steadily towards her church,

a high cold stone. Later they will bring her back.
Inside and overhead, a massive stained-glass
scene of angels and shepherds; it carries
no current message: the trumpets held up

are silent; the bedded sheep whose heads
are turned to look do not listen
to the hiss of cars on the street — it was all so
long ago! Things are different now.

The angels tilt their heads, their ruby lips whispering
a rainbow of sunlight across a worn warm-wood pew.
There, this day, Red Lady will sit to talk
quietly to God, or perhaps to listen.

*Red Lady Goes Shopping*

After listening for the voice of God
around the preacher's rolling talk,
Red Lady is filled with new
emptiness. The angels do not

move down from their high loft to put soft
trumpet-music in her ears. The sheep
begin to stare. The colors of the shepherds'
robes rise to gaudiness; and closer,

the smooth pews seem hard and bare.
At the end, she finds that she has found
nothing: a passing cloud cuts even the
sparkle that earlier had hugged the air. She rises,

a red cloud. Her shoes take her
across the walk and to her car, empty.
She drives to fill herself with
something from the store. There, a jaunty

music pulls her buggy down and up the long
rows of boxes, bottles, bags; cool
fluorescent lights bounce a hard new hope
from brightly colored cans on shelves.

She wants for a brief moment to drop to her knees
and weep like a child but her black
shoes take her farther, to where she looks at
pieces of butchered sheep stacked red under

cellophane; they take her to a small
mountain of green peppers and red tomatoes that
beg to be squeezed; they take her past the
crispness of celery; they take her past the firm

thump of melon, the rich gold of pears and Christmas
oranges. Finally, she buys a *Cosmopolitan*:
she likes the way the woman on the cover
has done her hair.

*Red Lady Does the Beach*

The sun cuts to the mustard near noon when
Red Lady decides to do the beach. High overhead,
small clouds move quickly, pushed roughly to the east.
Some gulls cry; they wing like black shot carried hard

by the stiff wind. Grasses hold the sand
tenaciously in a miser's grip of roots;
they bend, bend, nodding methodically in the wind.
Ahead, low breakers crash, muted, slow: the thin

sun cuts through the air, cuts through the wind,
cuts through the far-off cry of the gulls; it
bakes down into the sand, warms the thin
surface of the sand, brings an end to the last

warm part of summer. Beyond the variable swell of
breakers, the water far out heaves and rolls,
heaves and rolls; it glistens, listens; it hears the
thud and hiss of waves, the thin long keen of the gulls.

Red lady's blanket laid out makes a bright
plaid plot, a bold eye to the sky; it says, this
is where I am. See me. She reclines, feet
towards the waves, head

towards the grasses, the crook of her left arm cast
carelessly across her eyes for shade.
The waves thud on the beach, a timeless hammer
full of acceptance. In her self-imposed blackness,

in that blackness of self,
warmed by the small sun, her curves
fit down into the curves of the sand. The gulls
start to sound like the far-off

trumpets of angels. The wind
moves her long hair. She feels
drawn up by the sun, drawn up on a
thin spindle of yellow fire. She dreams.

*Red Lady Dreams*

In her dream or in some dream, Red Lady
floats effortlessly across a far-flung field. She
moves through weeds but does not feel them. She
moves through grasses but they do not

touch her. She comes to a
soft place near a river, where pebbles are
old runes; they spell out her name, they
have something deep to tell her. They

sing her a thin song, light as air,
a deep trill, about all of everything.
Red Lady nods in her sleep, rich in a
dream-textured understanding. She

looks up then and finds a wooden plowshare; it
splits the soil of a fertile field. On this
field there is red on the left, white on the right.
Where the plow has been pushed, or pulled, it

casts up red on the right, white on the left.
An oriental farmer in a conical straw hat comes to her;
he tells her that when one plows with this plow
there is no turning back. The rough

wooden handles are sun-warmed; their curves
fit to her hands. In dreaming, like not-dreaming,
Red Lady feels the sun against her cheeks;
the wind caresses the soft angle of her jaw.

*Iris Rising*

This thin story trickles slow as cool blood
through small veins. It has no smell;
it is not a hairy bearskin. It is not
as profound as the far-off chatter

of wheeling gulls whose flight
stitches the sky and holds the clouds
high with a thread of wind. But sometimes
life seems spare, thin, faithless.

When not-dreaming, Read Lady is confused:
there are so many little things that make her forget
the plow, the work of a life;
forget the clean and fantastic sense of

red spilling onto the white, the white
spilling onto the red. I wait now for the
great axe, which, when it falls, will split me
with a massive thunder, releasing the steaming

black horse, huge oily engine of progress.
But while I wait, the gulls just soar and soar and
cry thinly against the wind. Listen: it is
your quiet dream, Red Lady, that will carry me

to the soft-throated still voice of a deep iris,
flower formed lovingly from the most perfect purple;
your dream will carry me to the place where bees
put thick honey to the nest in an empty head.

# Construction Techniques

1.

I could pepper you now like Archie did
with dates and weather
reports: he didn't miss a stroke
or if he did, then just a few.

A squall coming, maybe, or a breeze —
nice and warm, crocuses are starting to
pop up, later the grape hyacinths
mouse-ear cress does fine

all winter: all winter, even puts out
little white flowers to match
the intermittent little snows
so: getting more to the root

of the thing, it's good to
step back a notch or two and
peruse the thing: think about it;
take rough measure

of its girth and estimate its height, the
rotundity or lack thereof and
(with luck) after a while get down
to brass tacks: scope out

the problem and begin to con-
sider the pros and cons of
various types of
possible solutions, as if

it is a problem. It might be
for example just a condition, a slim

fester of reality, a thing
that is, which needs

no solution. Color
for example. Or a sound.
We're more likely to associate
such things with particular things,

something unique to us
as individuals. Color is
you know, just color and we (or most of us)
see it in raw form and in

delightful mixtures; photons
arrive spread over a good wide range
of wavelengths and then by golly
the brain does things with those inputs

like crazy, assigning pixels to shapes
recalled but
it can go the other way as well,
I've seen: see

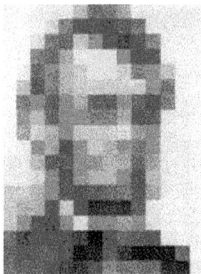

not so many pixels * and yet
your pallid jelly-blob can still
integrate like mad
isn't that

purely wonderful? It's good
to give attribution when you can. So many
don't do that. Think this:
someone had to do the work

to make the thing from
something else and that takes
time, work, energy, foresight, some
planning, why not

let others know you know that's true.
And
the weather today is
stunning: creeping up towards

70, sun out full, plants
are taking deep sighs
of relief: the OK, return to
goodness kind, not the

topographic variety. Today
you can almost hear the buds swell.

2.

Found
a great line today: *I forgot*
*that I forgot you.* By poet
Linda Parsons, in Princess Visitation,

*Reckon Review*, February 22, 2021
and I hope
these details don't detract or distract
you: this is

my attribution for her lovely words:
they remind me
I've forgotten many things and
with well-directed effort I might remember

some of those forgotten things:
items: times: events: some particulars
can be remembered sometimes (but not always)
and can be assigned as truth: the brain fills in

so many gaps and verges (Roald
Hoffmann said that and you should
look it up). * I observe
many newscasters and politicians

start their spiels with "Look," or "See," while I
prefer So: as if
to start anew while their mission
differs a little — it is, I think, to aim

the viewer towards some hoped-for
shared vision, thus the verbs but
in any case, let's just move on.
In *Tape for the Turn of the Year* *

Archie's lines were so short they almost
squeaked: just one word
in many cases whereas, look, mine
usually are a tad

longer.
But not always. See,
I find that funny.

3.

Like our two dogs, each on a leash:
they pull
like crazy almost always
in opposing directions so the lines

get crossed over, sometimes
tangle yet always
pulling in some of several
and varying directions, my

that is so hard on the hands, even the
arms and shoulders. The keyboard
is more benign yet still
imperfect. The fingers now

for example, but more particularly the
knuckles and crusty
finger-joints and even the little
bone-joint way at the base of the

left-hand thumb come to realize
they've been worked over: the aches
set in. So let's try "now"
instead. That's probably better than

look or so or see: but just now
a brown thrasher smacked the window hard
and when I looked out to see
what the heck was going on he had

taken position on a dogwood limb
below the window: rattled
his cage I bet; just perched there
a good long while, thinking

things over, con-
templating maybe his lucky stars: he did not
break a neck, for example — his
in particular.

Eight minutes later he's still
perched there but at least he's moved
to a different branch. Perhaps
the dash damaged his noggin. I'm

fascinated to find that noggin also is a
small cup or a signaling protein involved
in embryonic development,
or a gill, a unit of volume, equal to

a quarter of a pint and that's a
pretty small beer. Or a con-
struction technique, in which
bricks are used to fill vacancies

in a wooden frame. That shows
context is so important.

4.

Context is
where you start from: it doesn't matter
if a short race (just a sprint) or a
cross-country run, you get ready and

get set and go, that is, start, and it is
from a place
you can name or describe;
the colors on your jersey (lurch

back: red and gray
at my high school
where I ran track and cross-
country) and how then we stood

leaning forward, poised at the start-line,
heart starting to ramp up, take a deep
breath, and another, get ready
that's context

for action that follows: the too-quick
initial pace, then carefully settle
into the slightly slower race-pace,
getting synchronized just right, the arms

with the legs with the
breathing with the heart and
when all that's good, you're good
as you're going to be. Sometimes

a runner from the other team is
there, not far in front of you so you
drill down and get determined to
beat his ass. And do it.

That's context too — all the stuff
around the thing
you actually want to talk about.
Thirty minutes now

after the hearty bird-thump and
the thrasher's still
perched in the dogwood, he
must have rung his bell pretty good.

Around here, his type is
less common than robins doves blue-jays
chickadees English house sparrows
wrens and insert

robins again, this time of year
they're everywhere, flying low
and hard, plumping up
fast as possible: orange
and black jerseys, white tail-trim

5.

Now, look, see, so
this Black Lives Matters swell
seems swell to me — I'm fascinated,
hope it goes well, will try

to help in my little way: it's
long overdue. Why

we can't do better is beyond
me: or I guess we aim to do better

and I hope we will, so saying
can't do better is a negative-space
way of saying we can and sure should
that's

more context anyway. But there's
so much more available: the Jim Crow laws
were positively dreadful (see here how
positive contrasts with negative)

and that (ambiguous) puts stress and strain
on the system until

it breaks if something doesn't stop
so, hey, I'm happy to help

grease the wheels. Sort of
out of
my historical bailiwick
but so what. I lived

two years in Ghana, have
some respect for that, have
a lot to learn here and we're even
trying to figure out, what it means

exactly
and how
best to help
exactly

for example in my church: I'm
on the vestry now and was
last year and will be
next year

and right now we're
at the starting line: getting
ready to get poised
for purposeful changes,

maybe we can
make a difference, get things right
(er), sure
we can't make it perfect but

we should be able to make things
better. Need more
context:
need to:

step back,
take its measure

like:
something old
something new
something borrowed

something blue —
more than 35 years ago
when I served in the Peace Corps in
Ghana, now that

was a serious
experience: a blend

of old and new: tap
that reservoir as much as

rationally possible: or borrow it
I guess, if,
when worked with, I put it back
in good shape, and better

if possible. Really
Volta Lake was blue, blue. I learned a lot and
some of it might be useful for
more than context if

I can extract it
correctly and accurately — don't
bring in too many
gaps and verges, plaster

cracks truthfully
stick with it
like oatmeal
or grits, we can celebrate

a new beginning
(but hold the balloons please; we need
to save helium, it's getting
scarce)

6.

Not long ago I found a news article
on how to make bricks
from waste plastics and sand and the sand
probably could be made from

crushed glass bottles — glass is a problem
in its own right because
it is so cheap: it is
scarcely worth recycling whereas

plastics remain
    a Big Donkey Problem
which needs solving but if
if (if) one can heat

plastic fragments mixed with sand and
extrude bricks, why
that might solve several problems
at once but I'm sure, too

it will create a few new ones so
someone really needs to scope it out:
align
relevant context, do the calcs,

run the numbers, check'em twice: glass
for example can wear out
an extruder's auger, what
to do about that, that's

a pricy potential problem and ask
are plastic bricks durable enough
and strong enough to use in home
construction, or at least good enough

for sidewalks, parking lots
and terrace walls, we need those things too,
especially if the cost is low compared
to the cost of making conventional bricks

from fired clay: that process
takes so much energy, produces
so much $CO_2$
what a mess

7.

I'm putting
a lot of faith, maybe too much, in
technological progress: things like
3D printing, quantum

computing, artificial intelligence,
how to treat sewage
to better specs with novel
nano-flocculation agents, how to stabilize

high-performance solar cells, how to
make wind turbines
safer for birds and bats, and how to avoid
neonicotinoid pesticides, they play

so badly with birds and bees
and lots of other
useful insects: forget for a moment
about mosquitos: I guess they help bats

and maybe swifts and swallows
but also they can carry

malaria
yellow fever
dengue fever
chikungunya

equine encephalitis (east and west)
Nile virus and La Crosse and
Japanese encephalitis: maybe they can fix
such problems with CRISPR

and a gene drive, I
don't know, there's
just too much context
to grasp, too many

construction techniques:
be brave, help
how you can, not
if

# Now, but Not Yet

1.

Bank paper, blank sky, a blank mind —
it's a blankety-blank day

hard, cold and bright. Beetle pupae
like swollen rice grains are motionless

frozen in dark soil a foot down — the grass is iced
clear through. On the patio peach tree out back

two leaves remain
and two leaves only, wavering but clinging —

ready to go yet still attached
by particular cells at particular ends of particular twigs.

Each leaf, each thing,
withered or not, is

for a moment
in its particular place.

2.

A mathematician who knows physics
or a master of physics who knows math

after much contemplation came to believe
something new about time. Now he thinks

time does not exist. He thinks
time is just the way we see

from frame to frame, each frame
a universe, with all universes

existing at the same time: clearly
we could be anything we want —

pick the path forward. See,
now others are beginning to agree: their mouths

make happy little ohs, their heads
are nodding: the idea makes sense, they think,

the equations work; at last
certain loose ends can be tied up.

So put that in yer pipe and smoke it.
Wanna dance?

3.

Let it be true
for a moment. Knock

dead ash from the pipe, turn
the head and look back

over the shoulder. What's that,
you say, I see — ?

For the first time in many years
I see a child reading a book

by candlelight: the candle is white;
it provides

a flickering yellowish light in what otherwise
would be dark, yet it is enough to see

the child seems to be a boy;
he seems to have blond hair; his eyes

seem purely attentive to the book he holds.
The candle's flame

generates a bit of heat, which melts
the wax beneath the wick; the wax

is drawn up the wick, to the point
of combustion; carbonaceous molecules

leap to the air, seemingly joyous; they unite
with molecules of oxygen and give off

light and heat: these molecules do this
until the wax runs out, if the air

is present in surplus.
I ask

how many universes does it take
to capture this wavering scene?

4.

Something whispers "Now, but not yet."
Like the nude

descending the staircase *
forever we are trapped

in a cubistic landscape: each instant
grips the next.

# A Matter of Fact

1.

It's Wednesday morning. The coffee is hot
and ready to go, the laundry's done,
the dishes are wiped and put away, the house

is quiet, poised like a non-rung bell.
Clam clam clam — such a busy rhythm
near silence, modulated intermittently by the cat

coming and going here and there and flopping
her heavy body down
where ever she wants. On my right,

a copy of *Selected Poems*
by William C. Williams; it allows
opportunity for occasional

emergence of inspiration. On my left,
the keyboard; it allows for occasional
escape to the internet —

periodic searches
for information I don't need
to live. Scrape a Texan they say

you'll find Oklahoma blood. And I have
no idea where that came from, or
why it's here.

2.

Everything worth anything crosses the river,
mythologically speaking: it could be
the Rio Grande, or the Red River,

or the Amazon, or the long
river with the long name, the one
containing so many i's and s's

(sighs and stresses), the long one
meandering north to south,
or (help us, please!)

the gloomy River Styx — :
it doesn't matter. Inevitably I find it
the same: it comes back or loops around

to ideas or beliefs or bodies or
            things begging
for nothing more than a

pathetic level of redemption;
a level that might be had
by crossing running water.

        Things

come out the other side
glistening, shaking off
wet drops flying, even as oceans

heave in their rocky beds
tossing froth, making
low and sloppy noises.

Know this: we still honor the pitiful few
who crossed in flimsy ships: not
for them, but for their thoughts: odd

notions spiked like steel rods
in fevered brains — incoherent
red-rimmed visions of how things ought to be

somewhere in a new land.
Sanctimoniously speaking
in platitudes, these gaunt pariahs still were filled

to overflowing with
righteous gumption and grand ideas.
Later, heading west, wagons

creaking and groaning,

pulled by oxen, dumb eyes,
their slow heads down.

3.

Desperation — a scraping
down to the deepest layer. Knowing
one can't make a silk purse from a sow's ear,

attached or non-attached, it's a dead
certainty. Cut
deep as you like, the DNA

won't change
under the blade: you're who you are

nothing more, often less.

Dear God, let me rise
at least for a moment
above myself.

4.

It's a busy day — things crowd in
nuzzling like wet dogs, each
begging for a bit of individual love. I think

spring flowers, the first
blue crocus; the first
blades of baby grass

but it is too early for that.
More snows
are still to come, the sky

thickens as I watch two juncos
fritter briefly in a bleak oak,
longing for south. Turning

back to one of the jobs at hand
I wonder: can we use multispectral Lidar
to tell us spring's arrival?

Would we believe it
if it did?

5.

On some matters one can't turn back.
The task
is to bring things out — display them,

fresh vegetables and fruit,
crisp and sweet
or tart enough to curl the tongue

lovingly of course.
I say this
as a small matter of fact.

# How to Take Off

1.

Fallow land, autumn, a sketchy sky
infused with thin clouds, lined up or scattered

anywhere at all nowadays
since it is

the electronic age. Or some say
the digital age. Can you imagine

packaging music in bits and bytes?
Like dots and dashes but

more succinct: boiled down and distilled
to ones and zeros, back-to-back in strings.

Nothing down that avenue, I think,
So, put'er in reverse, back up and let's go

chk out the next alley, graveled.
Whoops. Yesterday I wandered

through the strawberry bed. Their green leaves
crowd it, taking over:

they must like the horse manure
provided in summer. Now

a minor wonder, they're pushing out
even the Bermuda grass.

This fall I'll cover them with straw;
wheat-straw. Let it come down on them

thin as rain, but more lasting
and less transparent. Giving:

opacity for winter.
It would be so peaceful to slip

back to bed, snuggle the pillow, pull
the blankets up and sleep.

Can't do it. Have to work today.
And rouse the kids for school. It's a shame.

Now, said that but what else
needs saying? Sometimes I can slam

words to paper but they're no good
without spice behind them

and spice is what I lack. Dangle
a carrot or show the whip and things

get done; else, one might as well
sit back and wait.

2.

Got a meeting for this morning at 0845
sharp: it has to do with fossil energy,
the project manager keeps his eye on things
in Washington D.C. and he lets us know

who said what to whom and why
federal money coming down like rain
won't happen this year

or probably the next.
Instead a drought
he says we need to do things

smarter this year, work in teams.
With that, the damned words fly
out of me like birds fly

in autumn as a group, moving
like slow dots across the sky.
The grayness of this grainy day

makes me think November.
It's the kind of day
a black bear gets up, stretches and crawls

from her den and stands there sniffing
the air sour as mulch from autumn; see,
she shakes her heavy head

to clear cobwebs; sees
goldenrod and iron-weed, and knows
it's time: the last few days

have come again, it's time
to dig the last oily grubs, to rake
the few remaining berries off the bush, time

to galumph slowly, with her rolls of fat,
to the orchard, to strip
the low fruit and eat the windfall

the yellow-jackets left
littering the ground.

3.

A radical change in plan: scrap
the hypothetical bear — I hear
they wander now through Gatlinburg,

tipping garbage cans and raising Cain —
no small trick given we're in the Bible belt
tight enough to make you squeak.

Every other corner's got a spire,
the first
church of this or that — often long names

for small facilities. But that's
the way they like it: first in prayer and first
in sin, and that's the state the country's in.

No worse
I guess
than moose in Maine.

4.

Circle back
to William Carlos Williams; I need
to re-learn

how to surprise; how to bring
and present a gift: so many hows
get left by the side of the road

on gravel or in weeds. Carelessly; things
some people don't give a damn about,
what's where. I swear

pick any place at all and begin
digging or poking around — ashes,
brick-bats, bits of glass, best if by water,

two if by land: and suddenly
you can find yourself —
leap and fly, strong muscles

pulling you up in the air, the wind
can't blear the incredible view, the road
just a thin ribbon below, the white-trunked

aspen bursting yellow in clots on the hills,
the huge sky

oh, take just a second to see it
impossibly blue.

# Opening

As a noun, it is at least a thing,
or a void in a thing, a place to start —
a thing through which one can exit
if you're in a place you don't like.

But study that: first, imagine
such place. Perhaps you got there
by doing something:
perhaps you can exit

by doing something. Or perhaps
by doing something differently,
or perhaps by not doing — an opening
perhaps too small to squeeze through —

a slender crevasse, a
scarcely visible
crack in the wall, something
that might admit

a slow drop
of water-truth now and again;
or a minuscule
shaft of light, just a few

random sparkles, smaller than a
far star against the black of space.
Oh, how time unwinds
like a kite-string wound tight

on a drilled-wood rod! Or is it
un-wound, as in to heal? Scabbed-

over, I find it
still inflamed;

warm to the touch, tender.
So the body tinder. As inflamed
or enflamed on a pyre upon death:
a condition permitting

a wholesome way out, a way
to exit, opening or no.
Yet opening thereafter:
to the possibility of afterlife;

or to the possibility of life;
or at least

to the possibility
of possibility.

2.

Or as a verb: to un-close or,
if not closed previously,
that is, from never open — then
spread out from a more compact

form: a soft exhale; a
controlled expansion, a gentle release
from compaction; a re-
laxation from a state of taut, to a

less-tense state. When I
close my eyes and look back
to the younger me, I shed
strange years. We learned

mostly alone or with a few others
and found more than enough
time: more than enough time
to look back, and time to

pause and look ahead. The old pin oak's
gnarled roots holding the sand in place
had hoary limbs great enough
to take our weight

high in thin branches. From there
when the leaves agreed to let us
see through we could see
far off, across the dune, the path

sometimes we took to wild
strawberries, or sassafras,
or pin-cherries, or
to the field of ferns. We named

things according to our worldly wishes
though some things had names
we learned and by choice accepted.
Paused now, looking back, it was

the learning, the accepting, and
the agreeing upon of names: it was
and still is our way of dominion;
the varnish to our knowledge; a thin

shining lacquer-layer of understanding
of things we think we know
and sometimes try to relay
to others.

3.

Scatter-shot: the rattle of small and
energetic stresses can make holes:
down like hail — (South, they say like hell).
Now, sometimes, I can see and say

uh-oh, I know what's coming next:

dry leaves scatter before a gale. Writing
long-hand and letting the dog
out into the back yard one might say
oh, please, oh, pen the gate. Now that's bad.

But be serious a moment;
or try at least. Spicy mustard;
or pickled jalapenos: the latter

add zing if diced and applied
sparingly on chili, or better if
they're stuffed with cheddar and cream
cheese, get wrapped in bacon and baked

sparing detail for a good meal
but it's detail that makes the world
go round. Think how boring
it would be if there were no details:

what if
for example, everything (ever-thin) was closed;
just closed, no opening: smoothed over, no bumps
pits dimples indentations dents

hollows or things like that that give
texture to the universe.
Thinking
this morning as I drove

to Knoxville, rain
beating the windshield: what if
the universe was smooth
as warm butter, not even

a little froth as the fry pan heats
          before
before adding
minced garlic, zucchini, yellow

crooked-neck squash, sliced
mushrooms, maybe a tomato
(diced; core cut out) seems I can't
lose those last five pounds

I'd like to lose; with age
comes decrepitude: it happens
to vehicles too, my (ex) Frontier
was developing a clutch

problem; those usually don't
result in catastrophic failure,
they just
fail slowly, getting worse

and worse until
you must do something about it:
get bold, buy replacement and figure out
best you can how to get the old one

out and the new one in, then there's
inevitable need to make adjustment;
that's fine
if you like to do that, or have to do that

because your financial status won't
allow another path: it's closed. I don't
like it, it's
a big bump.

4.

Reconsidering: perhaps I could
crawl through: working
down, on hands and knees as if
in supplication, presuming

rocks on knees not too bad
or if they were, then go prone,
wriggling if need be, constantly
from where now to when,

scrunching along until
        finally
a little light, a little open; all those
memories

surge back, rising
mist-like from cold muck,
like marsh marigolds, skunk
cabbage. They're

crisp and beautiful,
but such an odd place to stand.

What if
I had opened to desert instead?

Or to ponderosa pine, pinyon
juniper, or higher, to crisp, thin air,
Douglas fir and aspen?

Yesterday morning in the woods
behind our house at the base
of a loblolly pine I saw motion; a small
splash of red on something

black. It was
a pileated woodpecker, what
a delight; it made
the whole morning whole: everything

for a moment opened. The grand bird
worked up and around the trunk
stopping here and there to check
more carefully the crinkled bark.

Joy like that
is hard to come by;
it's worth waiting for.
God

or nature willing,
we should work or rest
to fill ourselves with that
each day.

# First We Might Start

with a few clean items dragged in
from last week's slippery world
of science. For example, neutron beam-time
took a big hit; something

went down; or, a fingernail-painting
robot now will do you
for less than ten bucks. Probably first
in California. And with respect

to Covid: honoring that
with a capital C, as that is
all the rage, PF-07321332
has a favorable off-target selectivity profile —

or at least, more than 120,000
scientists now have opportunity
to think so. But take time to compare members
now and 'member snow: close enough

in local parlance to get you
kicked back
into the biggun in '93, 'member that? It is
chilly today but not that cold,

frosty first but in the forty's now
and bright, so
take a moment: spin off here
into a different form. Something

a little looser, a bit more
casual, less snug, not
so tight. Maybe we can get there

by and by by adding a few lines to the stanza, or perhaps
by making the lines a bit longer, or perhaps by finding
an easy way to stretch things out, make them
limber; somewhat elastic, more flexible. We can hold

to conventional sentence structure for a while, at least
long enough the get the thing moving
        (moving a bit)
in the direction of choice. And choice

is the Big Daddy Starbucks for me and
probably for many, think about it
from the left and the right, then flip the bloomin' thing.
Choice is

the bottom thing
you're left with if you're going down
and the top thing
you're left with if you're going up, and

by choosing
up or down
you open
a new path.

And from all this
wanton dithering something might come: sometimes
that's how a thing starts, like
the Big Bang, 13.8 billion years ago, something

from nothing, or something
that seems like nothing, then
life on Earth, 3.8 billion years ago, more
or less, unfolding flower-like

from a tight bud.

2.

So gradually let's begin
making the turn: put the pole to the mud,
push hard the rear end of the punt the way
you don't want to go and
away you go, slowly

the other way. Odd how many
water-based images, metaphors, similes
creep into play, when
crawdad-like, we go
forward by pushing backward. That has

something to do with cause and effect:
action reaction resistance force,
probably friction in there too: if you feed
the puppy he'll follow you
home.

3.

I'm less optimistic about things
today. We're punting
too slowly; things are spinning
out of control, the feedback
loops are working day and night like a

unionized labor force: a blizzard
of un-ionized,
that is, not charged
things but
the momentum is built in: the ship
left port a while ago, we're out there now
rolling with the waves — not just bay-ripples,

the real things, hoot and gander (fox and geese
if the snow gets deep): pitching
now and again, rising and plowing
head on into the next wave, wave
after wave after wave
each one a little larger than the one before, the

sky is starting to darken (pointing), off there
to port; scud clouds
are starting to move in, the barometer

drops another tick.

Here are things that seem to me
likely to happen: probably
more large earthquakes, now and again, as
ocean water-weight redistributes; probably
larger-than-average or more-than-average

volcanos as the mantle settles a bit as
water-weight redistributes. We know already

more storms, more intense storms; upsets
in the hydrological cycle (maybe a punt-boat
is a reasonable metaphor after all)

and hard freezes when the jet stream gets
tangled up
with polar chill before
plunging south; and more arid parts of the world
getting more arid as soil dries due to
increasing soil warmth. We're still spreading

invasive species like mad; we're forcing
opportunities for new pandemics, fires, crop
failures, things

will just grind
more slowly; oil won't help,
damn
why

did we do this for our children?

4.

It's more pleasant
to put dark notions aside; focus
instead on the few good things
we can do today: put fresh

birdseed into the bird-feeder, forget
about problems caused by supplementing
calories given freely to select wildlife;
blow leaves

off the driveway with the gasoline-
powered leaf-blower, thus changing
where more decomposition should occur;
hoe weeds

around the collard plants in the raised-bed
garden, changing competitive dynamics;
sort
recyclables from honest trash, even though

glass and so many plastics can't be
recycled economically yet
look, we're all in
this leaky little boat together.

5.

First things first: perhaps
if we each drew back a bit, paused
a moment to let truth ooze in
we could start

doing things right.

# Revealing

## 1

If I should reveal myself —
for example, show my fears,
describe their origins, their odd
beginnings, the peculiar threads

holding one to another
snug and compact from the soft blurred
vision of youth — towheaded and owlish
from the beginning, and not so social

but with questions and ability to learn
a better way soon after making mistake
(but not so much in school, where
most useful learning happened

on the playground: such as:
when hurling acorns at opponents,
one hard to the cheek was enough
to make do). Noting to self: crying

did not does not change things much:
rather, tears can obscure
a fruitful path forward. Perhaps
filaments of memory will get pulled up

through time as away we go: gossamer strings
tied to odd things dangling; pulled up
and reeled in when one tries to relinquish hold,
for even if by so doing one fully fails

to expose self, a pallid larva:
alive but soft plump helpless

defenseless and useless until
maturation happens: the shell then hardens,

fluids get pumped to the wings; cunning
joints find proper articulation and
threads of developing muscles creep around
and attach interiorly

here and there
as genetically designed, to
interior surfaces of the exoskeleton
which supports its own iridescence

and externally, cicada-like,
multifaceted ommatidia.

2.

It is not clear
how many turns you'll need to make
on this path; how many setbacks
and hesitations before

ending up somewhere useful;
or if the end will be
useful at all: clots, roots and stones,
well-barbed berry-bush canes,

a few of which are still green and limber
but some from last year, gray and hard:
ready to snap if one applies
firm force by bending with two hands;

snap the thing

abruptly in twain. Two questions
and a wish do not provide
suitable support for a good poem —
they do not establish

an adequate framework, regardless
of fine words leading to and from the core.
One must bear down
more firmly: make sparks jump; put

the acrid odor of carborundum
to the air, until
the first glint of steel under the rust
appears. Skip momentarily

to *A Coast of Trees* * with nothing,
nothing, we turn
to the cleared particular: to the raw bits,
the nuggets, grains, and odd-bob

things found, scooped up and held dear,
undigested, unshared,
close to the heart until death.

3.

Revealing
requires one to shed cover.
And it requires
showing — effort more active

than shedding, more toward
explaining describing demon-
strating changes between
before and now and clarifying

(to the self in particular)

what just went down.

4.

Down
can be forever but it need not be
if one holds
tight to gumption. Down,

twisting a little
this way and that along the way,
sometimes making happen a
tentative wobble, a waver, a

deliberate slow-cantered hap-
hazard spin, the axis
flexible and immaterial
mostly. Rather, it's

the slowing, the coming to stop:
take pause there; take time
to inspect; do not take
the place lightly — it is there

for a reason. Respect
things you have done
relative to others; do not
disrespect others.

When the heart
stills to silence and each beat
calls an eternity
you can shrug

shoulders to shuck cover and rise,
diaphanous, humble, triumphant.

# We Can Dance

Amidst profusion, amidst
this wild riot of growth, living green is
punctuated
ferociously with yellow, orange,
blue, shades of lavender, a few reds.

Amidst this
raucous and unruly
splurge of color, swollen and
humming with life
there's so much more

than one green; it is, instead,
a multitude:
from dark to pallid
or pallid to dark; thus, life:
driven

to show, driven
to express itself
every way possible, saying
I am here, here I am,
ready

to live.

Just
a little water, some sun,
a few nutrients — something
to hold to, perhaps: a woody stem,
a bit of soil, or for lichens, even a wet

rock, or a branch, or a stone; oh, and
yes, something to hold with:
rhizoids, or specialized unbranched
adventitious roots,
knobby with hold-fasts, or roots

to penetrate, or hold by mere
chemical adhesion, requiring
just contact to start: to grip,
cling, clutch, grasp, or hold.

2.

Rising
silently from dark waters,
a nearly transparent jelly-blob: by slow

methodical
contracting and relaxing
a ring of muscle around the dome-

shaped delicate bell-body
of the jellyfish; pulsating as if
to rhythmic music, as if

to the slow rise and fall of tides,
matching the slow undulation,
the heave and swell

of waves;
an inch per second;
five feet

per minute — slow yet moving:
lacking brain, heart, ears, head,
arms, feet, legs, bones.

How could such creature
be the beginning of us?
It is

so fragile while we
are so rough, so anxious,
so bulky and hard-boned, so

perpetually dissatisfied.

3.

This is for all small creatures
crawling on or working under
rocks or through rich soil or rotting wood;

the hard-shelled or soft bodied,
jointed, segmented,
glistening or grub-like;

to the quick little
voles and moles that chase them;
the red-worms, the nematodes,

all creatures that creep or walk
with multiple stubby
legs and clasping feet;

the millipedes, the centipedes,
the sow-bugs and their ilk; and the legless
larvae, and the pupae

of moths and butterflies;
fireflies, longhorn beetles,
honeybees, wasps and flies and fleas.

To the thousands of little species:
the crickets, the grasshoppers,
even the ticks and mites; constantly

they try their best to live.

4.

And in fresh water, too —
all the fishes, of course: the minnows,
the bass, the bluegill, the northern hogsucker, even the eels.

The many kinds
of frogs; the salamanders,
the clams and the snails.

The water-penny beetles — all
272 species and a few
we may not yet know.

The congress
of caddisflies, dragonflies, damselflies,
mayflies, and the peculiar

whirligig beetles and water striders;
stoneflies, alderflies, dobsonflies, mosquitoes.
The long list

is growing shorter. And notice
we have not yet touched
the plants; and we have hardly touched

the mammals or birds. This is
our lost cause; our last chance
to learn the world: the fields,

the knobby hills, the knolls, and the tors
and the slopes and inclines; places
where the earth has pushed up

or eased down; places
through valleys, glades, forests;
mountains: by orogeny —

folding and uplifting,
especially along the edges
of continental plates.

The sedimentary and the metamorphic
types of rocks —
granite, quartzite, shale, limestone,

gneiss, marble, and
even the various kinds of coal —
the shining anthracites;

the bituminous, the lignite and peat.
We could go on
like this for a long time; for

thousands of years,
learning to learn:
learning to see and understand.

5.

Or perhaps you would choose
to turn inward, instead; choose to turn
to the words of Alexander Pope —
"the proper study of mankind, is man"

and "know then thyself." As if
such thing was possible. As if
such thing was true: our tangled lines
or lives or lies make twisted fishnets of our

convoluted understandings of self; thinking
we know when we do not;
presuming, assuming, and filling gaps.
Oh, the tizzy

when a thought-thing fails
to fit the gap: something
too large or too small, the wrong
shape or color; such as

loss of confidence when we first know
the thing won't fit: when for some
pure reason we know it's not
right: not suitable, not proper, it must be

rejected. Start the scramble
immediately to fix the hole; plaster
the disaster, everything is so
unsettled, even temporary

repair is better than no repair,
you think, while we dance,
and dance, pretending.

# Righteous Things

1.

Life flows up from life —
a thin sweet sap, frothing
at the edges. Always

the roots of the thing
ease down; grope through dark soil,
binding and bringing in

water, iron, phosphorus, nitrogen,
desire. These small things get mixed
in particular ways; they get worked

uphill to build
new things, make new life.

2.

Do this by yourself:
take one deep red rose
on a short stem

to the gravesite. Place it there
at an acute angle, alone.
For Mattie,

a wonderful dog. He was
respectful, kind, and
honor-worthy.

He made the world
smoother by living.

3.

Go on a slow
walkabout at a young age: say,
16 years or so; the purported purpose

then less than crystal —
the actual purpose
may not be known for years.

There's time then to make change,
time
to adjust direction. You can veer

to the south — keep the rising sun
on your left as you travel and imagine
how a young bird knows without knowing

when and how to migrate.
Imagine
how generations of Monarchs

know without knowing
when to move north and lay eggs
on milkweed leaves. The eggs

hatch to larvae, which then change
by chrysalis into butterflies
that know without knowing.

But the last ones know
when to flutter south
over 2,000 ragged miles

to overwinter on trees
in a forest
in central Mexico.

4.

From tension comes stress
and from stress, chaos.
Envision a teapot — one that whistles

sharp as a nail when the heat's on
and the pressure's up.

5.

It is difficult to learn
all the laws that pertain
to righteous things. Are we free

from moral defect? Are we
virtuous, worthy, and just?
If we do righteous things

do we make the world better?
Does it matter?

6.

Motion results from an upset in stasis,
from a change
in equilibrium. If I drive

carefully at night, not changing
my speed, things passing by let me know —
something's in motion.

7.

Honestly,
are you honest? Are you

courageous, generous, and fair
even when you don't want to be?

Have you ever cheated
at solitaire? Did you kick

the tires before buying the car?

8.

In late autumn even the birds
have troubles: they squabble
over the last seeds

in the birdfeeder and they shoulder
their ilk at the suet feeder
hung by a wire to the trunk

of a loblolly pine. Yes, the name
rolls from the tongue, a rich
lather of sound: like leatherleaf.

But the birds don't say it.
And they may not think it.
Being virtuous is difficult.

We do it
knowingly now and then and we pat
ourselves on the back when we do.

# From Where We Came

Up from the Olmecs in Mesoamerica, a tendril
thinning as it crept north — man, woman, child;
and north, from Tanzania and Kenya,
through Sudan and Egypt, north
into Syria, Turkey, Iraq and Iran,
trekking, hunting, reproducing, dying —

an unsteady but steady collective move
through ages: from Australia,
north into Indonesia, Viet Nam and China,
a wavering compass needle
from Africa to Spain, from Spain to France and Germany,
north to Denmark, Sweden, Norway, Finland — how far north

we don't know: yet north, tribes
splintering to smaller tribes
north, west and east, the collective
at times thin as smoke yet coiling north.

Several million years
working up and out of Africa; thirteen thousand years
or more in Egypt; more than a million years
in China, just fifty thousand years or so
in Australia. Take pause to count

the countervailing flows of people south —
from Siberia across the Bering Strait along the coast
of Alaska, the Pacific Northwest; and the
bend and wend of people east
and south along the coast into Florida; the back-curl
from Spain to Cuba, the flood of people south,
from Mongolia into China, the Picts

merging with Gaels, great sweeps
of intermingling people

from West Africa to the Caribbean;
Mayans merging with Spaniards in Mexico,
Japanese merging with Hawaiians — and the con-
flicted intrusions of people:
from Japan into China and from north Korea, south;
and south, from England into Australia, New Zealand
and South Africa, from Germany into Argentina —

in short, what are we

to make of such things? It is
human by nature to move out, human
by nature to push forth: writing
on clay tablets or on stone with stone
in hieroglyphics the history of an individual life,

or the lives in our communities: which king
begat which sons, which war
was won by which tribe, an arrow of time shot
from left to right or north to south
or from right to left, in
dozens of alphabets, whatever it takes to express
self to the world.

We know this: while thinning out,
curling up and moving
north or east or west or south through time

   inevitably

we gain, we lose

great pieces of ourselves: grand ideas
emerge, settle in, get dislodged and shucked off.

Genes are favored or get thinned out,
the hair, the skin, the color of eyes, the width
of noses, molecular
factors in the blood

of this great body, yet what else

comes and goes? We looked
back then from valley cave-lip out and up to stars
millions of years ago to constellations
signaling fate, and now from mountain-top
through telescopes to faint wobbles of light as planets
traverse the faces of their centering fires

yet always
the air, moisture-laden and hot or
raw and cold, going in
to lung and cell and out
dealing with the flood of data in, what new

gyres to interpolate
a honey-flow or burst of scent, the keen
of what we call a gull wheeling
the air and the thick reek of kelp and salt-splashed rock,
marsh and rot, frog-call, raccoon

looking back, a black-masked face as it
thin-fingers the water's edge. Desert
beardtongue, *Penstemon pseudospectabilis*, just one
of many species
bursting to bloom
in this particular case following a wet winter, local
to extreme — why call this species out
here, among millions as an example? Because

it is
like us
just one

of many types: variable, widespread; responding
to environment — the weather,
its nearest neighbors, the night-
time swoop and curl of cool air tumbling

down a canyon, attentive
to the flit of fly and bee, to the
whims of dawn, such
glory in early light this moment,
this small instant,
now.

# Wholly Intact (or in Fragments:

1.

So, with various examples: methods used
to emphasize, something's left
after frag-
mentation: whatever

is left is delineated —
by definition a fragment and
that's how this feels
today, cold, bright

February 8 and again
I can't see worth a damn
(lost the prescription
glasses

somewhere so now
for a time I depend
on cheap magnifiers. Everything
close up is sharp but

things farther than about
three feet are blurred; hell
why the
intraocular lenses don't

work both far and near is
beyond me but
let's get back to
today: starting now: it's roaring

towards spring: the Earth
wobbling a little
as it should and tilting
a little less each day as it

should, relative to its
axis, precessing in orbit, bringing
appearance of
longer days, warmth, sense of
wonder pending. Crocus

    maybe
or on the other hand or
      near the other end

of the spectrum, electrons
wobble a little, too, actually
more like flutter, as they

express themselves in
clouds of
probabilities, filling
their respective

orbitals with pure want: likely they feel
the delicate yet almost
irresistible touch of
quantum pressure: do

this thing or do that
according to what
feels right, well that
could be the big

secret of the universe:
no hesitancy no
uncertainty just go
with the flow.

A week ago
it wasn't like this: but
a week ago may not be a week
ago in electron-time — probably

it couldn't be so, so
step back
and
consider instead

the mule poems: * snugged
austerely and made real with
Kate and Silver brought to life
in one slender volume.

2.

Back briefly to the week
ago, before
the mule poems arrived: before
much of anything was allowed

to flutter, wander, waver
or express
some form of
uncertainty as to which

way to go or let go because
you know you have to

let go to gain new grip if
the goal is change

and sometimes
even when it isn't: sometimes
start a new way and
old patterns fall away

of necessity: no need
to knowingly
let go — just turn,
look back later and see

oh my, things
are different now: yes
they really are.
Well, when I was

just a tad sometimes I'd
hike to the swamp: dead trees, elms
perhaps, standing skeletons
but black-boned and beautiful

stink of marsh-gas rising with
each step from one mushy
tuffet to early spring-green tuffet
reeds or grass. I wish I could

see them again up close (and call them out
now by proper name) yet
stepping there from one
to the next insecurely (wobbling)

marsh grass roots burping
bubbles below one could
reach down, fondle the cold mud
and sometimes encounter

the smooth body of a pallid
frog overwintering
even as
spring peepers swelled and let out

astounding calls; and buttonbush
along bankside getting ready
and the brown-stained but clear
water exiting the swamp by

one route only: out. The water
entering by a dozen
secret springs: too shallow
for water lilies, OK

for cattails along the edge:
later I heard Dutch elm disease
accounted for swamp-tree death
but later still

I learned elms don't grow
if their roots are submersed in water
so: just: like: that: I'm caught
between two wrong things and

have no clear way of clearing
the mystery: were the dead trees
once not elms, or did the swamp
rise up from dry land to swallow

elms (and what it could) or
was death
due to something else — I can't
sort the facts not knowing

the facts.

3.

So see that's different.
I have wandered again:
the wobble
the flutter

takes me over, spills
my salt; I know a pinch
over the left shoulder won't
help. More lines

per stanza takes less space than
fewer lines per stanza so
go for it and while you're at it
do it daily. Rain today

and rumor of ice on Monday.
The pink swath on the monitor slides
up from Texas, northeast, Alabama
they say invading

artic cold from north yet in-
vading is not. quite. the perfect
word. Think on it. Would
encroaching be better

there's so much
crap in the world the world
is difficult to consider
on its own terms: it features

topographic weather
fronts oceanic shelves and
shores blurred again and
again by tides; hard-

pan deserts with
paloverde trees, golden suncup
creosote bush various
cacti skuttle-beetle-bugs, lizards

Elsewhere: sand-dune

grasses, blow-outs, sassafras
roots when dug up smell just like
root beer: pin cherry and back
to wet and early spring: skunk

cabbage; marsh marigolds: pussy
willow — all out and up
so early, early; and all crapless, too, all
things comfortably fitting in.

I can't tell you
how to live or if I did
you shouldn't listen be-
cause: think how

boring things would be: no new
thing under the sun except

by accident. So don't listen
or listen and don't act

waffle-flutter or
otherwise.

4.

This lying thing
is bad, bad
for those who do it and bad
for those that are then

supposed to make sense of it
or pieces of it, patched
cobbled stitched glued
to a useless whole: know

it is OK to say you don't know
when you don't know and
if you think you know be
really sure before you blat

with stern eyes, wrinkled
brow, lips down-curved slightly at
both corners although
lips and corners & angles jar

sensibilities — one being
soft moist and plump the other
not. But don't: creep back:
verify facts and check them

twice against what's what
there's the problem: dif-
ficult to discern identify cat-
egorize group separate or bin, put in

proper place. It's not easy
to find a new thing: it's easy
to rehash an old thing, pre-
tend it's new or: worse, think

it's new and spout it
as truth but you know
we hardly know squat
almost everyone goes

instead by easy feel.

5.

Cats, rabbits, ferrets
hamsters bats
can carry Covid: so can mink
and dogs and deer. We fare worse

perhaps because we're more
plentiful: easy spread and gullible
one must add — this is an example
where truth might

win out if we can just
stick with it, let it burn
out when it runs out
of easy hosts: try not to share it

back and forth between
those things and us: be-
tween with each step
wobbling a little with re-

spect to genes. What
works is what will work
for it — if it can't it can't, it then goes
south: and with respect

to bounce-back
when it works. Like laser tools
bounce-back works if you
know the speed of light

which we do mostly with some
degree of precision: just
a little flutter, maybe
at the end: 299792458

meters per second — here
insert approximately:
well, viruses can't replicate
that fast but obviously

they do it fast enough: and repli-
cation would have different
units unless you choose to
work it out in nanometers of

new DNA or RNA formed per second:
so there you have it. Slap
on a mask keep reasonably
far apart wash your hands

get a vaccine when you can
later it will
probably work out. Expect
more: you know

science is social
and in quick flutters we got
Gamma, Delta, C.1.2,
Omicron and more.

6.

If you choose to live
well and put
your heart into it
you can get

a lot done: no done thing
is perfect—that's
opinion so you see right
here I'm telling you

how to live: don't
listen, don't do what I did
it's been done, so do it
differently. What

the hell: you have: just: one:
so bang it
to your satisfaction,
warm milk

oatmeal cookie. I like
to rise early, earlier

than sun-up, up
when I can but now

hitting (getting) old I don't
so much although it's still good
when it happens. The dogs
help make it so

I guess
other things help too
maybe
the whole world helps

7.

Funny how
a cold front pushes south
and east even as trouble slides
north and east, sort of a

double whammy maybe:
the probability of ice
is looking up but don't
take that chance to Vegas; our trees

could take a hit — last time
ice brought down our big
weeping willow: chain saw
made pieces, lugged to the

curb for pickup. And
    it was gone
as far as we were con-
cerned; gone

except for carbon cycling.
And dents
in the yard where the
big trunk fell; and roots.

but that's then: now
we have several big lob-
lolly pines;
big'uns and if

one of them fell pointing
top away from the prevailing
wind well we'd
have a mess: something

would get crushed, the shed
at least, or perhaps
our sunroom, or a bedroom
or two of course it de-

pends on which pine and in
response to which
kind of external pressure: even ice
could do it I get

nervous about the possibilities
so many things could go wrong and
yet for years they've been fine,
fine, adding

a foot or two of height each year, they're
more than two feet in diameter
already: present
tense

I will listen
for tree-groans tonight: for
rifle-shots of big branches
coming down

consider wholly: probably
no surprise it sounds like holy:

The Christmas wreath goes down
the floral replacement
goes up and all the while
centering happens: circle, that thing

greening. As if wreathing was weeping
holding hands; sprigs wired tight
to the ring: yet dancing independent.
Many species of plants

and animals have deep dependencies
and beautiful Latin names con-
sider *Haematoccocus zimbabwiensis* —
five

syllables. Five: as if
counting meter I have no idea if
this critter de-
pends on some other critter, it might

or might not but others do, con-
sider:
the yucca and its moth, sharks
and pilot fish crocodiles and

plover bird ants and *Acatia* trees
protozoans and termites clownfish
and anemones and
lichens of course

and hundreds of other
pairs or triads: they are
so numerous and so uniquely functional
and so necessary: consider

even birds and holly:
So be holy let life stream
thru you
today

8.

Being outside
a polar vortex is better
than being in it: it's 60 below
in Montana and upper Michigan

other places like that but
most animals don't like that
which brings one
to question: do animals

act holy? Clearly
they act wholly, doing things
well to live if they don't
they won't but

holy's different, in part
if one is wholly this thing or that

the one is pure and that's
holy: just the sense of

life flowing up and through
(not so much
in a vortex but with a little
spin: maybe)

Last night I dreamed
again — one of many in which
students were there in some form: some
almost listened, most

did not; and like usual
I could will myself to float
gently down stairwells, not touching
the stairs, or down from a rooftop,

or from high on a ladder, using
no rungs just:
stepping off and willing: farther or gentler
just took more will maybe that's

another lesson,
me telling you
how to live. Remember don't
is next door to won't

Presumably
dinosaurs died from the Great
Impact of an asteroid slam-
ming near the Yucatan Peninsula

(but maybe a comet; odd
how details can matter
so much (like rain-glazed red
wheelbarrow white chicken;

Comets and asteroids
come from different places and differ
usually in chemical composition but
such details didn't

matter much to dinosaurs.
Didn't
or couldn't
Maybe turtles and alligators

escaped: they seem
gnarly boney
primitive too — know how to
hunker down and wait it out.

probably not lizards))

9.

But
back to living:
We all want a well-
lived life

whatever details that entails: doing
good, somewhere
along the line, not being a butt
all the time

perhaps only when needed but
that varies
of course: a drill
sergeant might need to be

rough all the time, it's
tough to tell. At least
I've never had my life
seriously threatened by

anyone except by my own
dumb actions, mostly
teen-time got better later
that's likely true

for lots of people, how
about you? You want
a life well lived? How
(won't tell)

Some con-
tractions can mess you up I get
flummoxed almost by its and it's
despite

how many times I look it up and
golly, I had a tough time
with girl spelling it gril
in second grade and still

tough it out with cereal
biscuit got broccoli at last
but not circuit it
has the extra i and I

tell the wife she should know
what I'm thinking. Just
details. Like decals
or worse tattoos, can you

imagine what a big one
put on at eighteen will look like
at 80, wrinkled saggy skin and
blurry faded ink and besides

things change
example: in the way you think
first care less
about some things then care

later a lot — links con-
nections to family and long
looks down the road things
speed up, watch

more carefully for bumps.

10.

Some dogs know
some details but mostly
smells
our Catahoula mix is a

mess: she talks a lot and
barks a lot, chunky portly
smallish for her size: her first
line of defense is to

rear up on her hind legs, push
with her two
front legs her favorite
thing is dinner. Pretty much

the same for the other dog but
she's not so talky generally does not
defensively rear up. Now how
we get to where we need to from here, can it

be details? like color, over-
all shape, some measure
of rotundity, height, the way
ears flop or flap or not; like

last week when I replaced our old
(light + fan) in the bathroom
ceiling with a new unit, it worked fine
except

earlier there were two
switches one for light
and one for fan but now one
switch does nothing and

the other turns on and off
the light and the fan
together: dang:
I did everything I could

to do it according to the
(not-so-detailed) directions: black
ink on cheap white paper to represent
red black white green I know

where the green wire goes
at least
that detail is surely important; maybe
they all are and if

it ever works right
again I'll let you know; could
celebrate with bubbly
OK

We did that (wife and I)
last night in comfy
chairs not far from the fire
(place; gas; logs — celebrate

And it was so good: just
talked about the day exploring
a few details / she's looking
through a trunk of old letters

from family: father, grandfather great-
ones and not just males the names
sound so much alike to me: Sis and
Sista for example (Nashville:

don't say r's the same way
others do, we're different
and some had multiple names like
Sista Hazel grandmother

or maybe multiple names
and titles: it would help me to see
a flow-chart: who
was connected to who and

and how and some of those
letters go back to 1905, chit-
chat like what we do now but now
we don't usually write it down

in letters anymore: the scrawls
difficult too — had to look hard
to decipher some words
although the words

   in many cases

were not so hard. The ink
fades too
like memories; a few

stay sharp but can change

stay sharp
as long as you can you can
listen to that
I think    )

11.

Wholly intact
or in (fragments: still some
of the message comes through
not a rip-

roar lightning stabbing
dark clouds leaving
temporary stains on the retinas
more like

bits pieces chunks or hunks
(not masculine although
they might be: jammed
German

shards work better
for pottery glass things
fragile but not
fragile

like a
butterfly snowflake: fragile like
stoneware, tempered
by heat — rather work

hard to be holy put down
the gun don't
grab for a knife you can
do it

other ways; maybe
hard to parse but try.
Briefly to the dogs again (see 10
love to tussle with a

small blue-and-white basket-
ball they found and de-
flated; it's ripped

almost in half and when the bigger
dog gets it the smaller dog
tries and usually
fails but when she's

lucky she gets it and keeps it
away from the larger with a
counter-clockwise
spin maneuver: every time: it

works to some extent con-
sistently but not
identically: if she would
just listen I'd tell her to try

the other way now and again
don't be so
perfectly consistent, go clock-
wise (looking down) instead: but she won't

or can't, it's built in, don't you see,
my, so many
apostrophes and commas
so close together; but step back

when the dogs come in from a
hard play down they go;
wish
I could nap like that.

12.

See, we're pulling closer
not to worry
about speed or lack
thereof all roads will take you

someplace if you
just try: stake out

a landmark to help keep tabs
at least a little on where
: you are : wholly
or in fragments keep

the faith in truth that's
about all we have
in this
    odd life


        )

# How Long is Long Enough?

1.

Like on a strip, tight
enough to make the jaws
ache; turn; turn it hard
to make short lines one

after another, he did it

so might I, yet
that's not the style I want
this time: it's good enough
to start with, sure, but

later, lines should roll out,
get longer; they'll need flex to capture
so many things connected, long
lines as if DNA strands. Didja know

if the DNA in just one of your cells was
unfolded, laid out end to end as straight strands,
it would reach six feet. And if
you did the same for all DNA for all the cells

in your body, it would stretch 67 billion miles,
that's 150,000 round trips to the moon.
Now that's a lot of skinny stuff, far longer
than wide. But this poem will not be that long.

It's just long enough
to link a few things, only long enough
to get things going—
to connect or link.

2.

Linking, after all, is just
a process; conceptually joining
one thing to another, by logic
or jump

of inspiration, to something else close by,
possibly related. Pine trees
for example, more than a dozen kinds—
loblolly, Ponderosa, jack, Eastern white,

longleaf, red, Monterey, mountain pine—
the list could go long and yet
these trees are linked
first by being trees, second by being

a particular kind of evergreen tree,
a conifer: a member
of the pine family: daddy pine, momma pine
and so many

urchins, some close and some
not so close, of course. It's all about
being, after all. And sense
of proximity

in time or space—isn't that a doozy?
I wonder sometimes why my lines
by themselves want to break out in
sets of four: the magic number

should be three but that seems
too short; sets of four
feel more cohesive, and
Lord knows, I need that. Wander

whither, wither, to what
aim or goal?
So if for example you steady up and aim
for a thing, you might

or might not get there—
but at least you might generate
sense of purpose
by choosing links and that

might not be a bad thing but
let's really get down
to the nut of the thing: to
brass tacks, in action terms

where the ball
meets the racket, presses
firm against the taut strings,
rebounds hard as if

with a life of its own it sails
back the other way, wind
or no, all according to the angles
and force applied. So

do you believe in life
after life? Have you had
one of those not-so-rare
near-death experiences?

I'm pretty sure I came close
upon almost drowning when
rafting and the raft flipped
in Maytag, a class five

churner in the North Fork Yuba River
the burbling sound of
bubbles roaring in my ears as water
roared around rocks and I

barely got my ass out of that
problem. But here's a different thing:
as a graduate student in a research
facility, one of the summer-program

faculty members died flat out
in a downstairs hallway, massive
heart attack, and several
minutes later, I, upstairs

in the autoclave room, saw him
clear and certain and he
did not say but was confused, not sure
what in hell happened. And me too.

And I'm not sure yet
where to link that.
Or if I should.

3.

Getting back on course
is sometimes easy
but sometimes not: it depends
on many things, the subject

of course, the intensity
of beliefs, the various
angles of thought. There's just
too many facts. Can some

be more true than others?
If they're all equal,
they're harder to link; it takes
persistence, fortitude, grit.

And still you're left
with a mess at the end. That's
life.
Well:

4.

having settled that
I'll cut back to the chase, to the
universal want to weave
this thing to that, building

a long reality from
raw suppositions,
from shorter things almost known or
strongly suspected

often for bad reasons.
We leap
hand over hand
to conclusions.

I do that, do you?

# Notes to Poems

*page 5*   * A.R. Ammons. 1974. *Sphere: The Form of a Motion.* W.W. Norton & Company, New York, NY. 80 p. ISBN 0-393-31310-7.

*page 13*  * W.C. Williams. 1985. *Selected Poems.* Edited and with introduction by Charles Tomlinson. A New Directions Book, New York, NY. 302 p.

*page 34*  * L.D. Harmon. 1973. "The Recognition of Faces." *Scientific American* vol. 229 issue 5.

*page 35*  * R. Hoffman. 1990. *Gaps and Verges. Poems by Roald Hoffman.* University of Central Florida Press, Gainesville, FL. 89 p. ISBN 0-8130-0943-X.

*page 36*  * A.R. Ammons. 1965. *Tape for the Turn of the Year.* W.W. Norton & Company, New York, NY. 220 p. ISBN 978-0393312041

*page 49*  * K. Puchko. 2016. "15 Scandalous Facts About Duchamp's "*Nude Descending a Staircase, No. 2.*" *www.mentalfloss. com/article/68674/15-scandalous-facts-about-duchamps-nude-descending-staircase-no-2.* Accessed June 22, 2021.

*page 75*  * A.R. Ammons. 2002. *A Coast of Trees.* W. W. Norton & Company, New York, NY. 66 p. ISBN 978-0393324105.

*page 94* * *The Mule Poems* is a 20-page chapbook containing seven poems by A.R. Ammons; it is illustrated by Joan Mansfield and was copyrighted in 2010 by R.A. Fountain. ISBN 0-9842102-0-2.

# About the Author

Arthur Stewart's poems have been published in more than a dozen national and regional poetry anthologies and in various literary and scientific magazines, including *Rattle, Journal of the American Medical Association, Lullwater Review, Big Muddy, New Millennium Writings, Bulletin of the Ecological Society of America,* and *Chemical & Engineering News.* He was a 1997 Tennessee Poetry Prize winner, a 2009 winner of the Wilma Dykeman Prize for essay writing, and a 2013 inductee into the East Tennessee Writers' Hall of Fame for poetry. He served as writer-in-residence at Michigan State University's Kellogg Biological Station, and has given science writing workshops for undergraduate, graduate and postgraduate science interns at U.S. Department of Energy facilities in Tennessee, West Virginia, Pennsylvania, South Carolina, Oregon and Colorado. *Logjam* is his ninth published collection of science-inspired poems.

www.ingramcontent.com/pod-product-compliance
Lightning Source LLC
Chambersburg PA
CBHW072352090426
42741CB00012B/3010

# Unwritten – Releasing the Past, Reclaiming Yourself

## A transformative guide to releasing conditioning, healing deeply, and embodying your truth.

*"This book changed the way I see myself. It felt like a conversation with a trusted guide, leading me through my own unmasking, showing me parts of myself I didn't even realise I was hiding. If you've ever felt lost in who you 'should' be, this book will help you find your way home to yourself." - Kiara S*

*"Finally, a book that doesn't just talk about healing—it walks you through it. With a perfect balance of science, somatics, and lived experience, it provides not just insight, but real tools for transformation. If you are ready to break free from past conditioning and step into your true self, this book is the map you've been waiting for." - Steph J*

*"Rarely does a book capture both the science of healing and the human experience of transformation so beautifully. This is more than a self-help book—it's an initiation into authenticity. Thought-provoking, compassionate, and deeply empowering, this book is a must-read for anyone on a journey of self-discovery." - Michael M*